# DEVIZES I
A PHOTOGRAPHIC

# DEVIZES IN FOCUS
## A PHOTOGRAPHIC TREASURE HUNT

ANDY ROSE

WEAVERN BOOKS

First published 2018

Copyright © Weavern Books 2018

All photographs © Andy Rose 2018

The right of Andy Rose to be identified as the author of
this work has been asserted in accordance with the
Copyright, Designs & Patents Act 1988

ISBN 978-1-78545-274-1

Published by Weavern Books
Vine House, 29 High Street, Corsham, Wiltshire SN13 0EZ
www.weavernbooks.co.uk

Text by Beverley Jollands
Design and production by Tim Jollands

Printed using a waterless process and bound in Great Britain by
Park Lane Press, Unit 11, Leafield Industrial Estate,
Corsham, Wiltshire SN13 9SW

FRONT COVER MAIN PHOTO
*St John's Church.*

FRONTISPIECE
*View down the Caen Hill flight of locks.*

TITLE PAGE
*Northgate Street and Wadworth Brewery.*

# CONTENTS

*About the Book*   7

*Introduction*   9

*A Photographic Treasure Hunt*   17

*Acknowledgements*   94

*About the Photographer*   95

*Competition Rules*   96

*The gateway at the end of St John's Court, which contains one of Devizes'*
*oldest surviving houses, concealed behind a later stone front.*

# *About the Book*

This book is intended to be both keepsake and challenge. All the photographs are of views and details in plain sight around the streets of Devizes, within about 1 km of the Market Cross. If you can identify them you are invited to fill in the form at the back of the book for a chance of winning a prize in our competition. The answers will be revealed and the winners announced at a prize-giving ceremony at the Wiltshire Museum, Long Street, on Friday 23 November 2018, after which the answers will be posted on our website.

Following the publication of our first successful treasure hunt, *Corsham in Focus*, in 2017, we were inundated with requests for more from those who had become addicted to tramping the streets seeking elusive details. Many told us that the exercise had opened their eyes to the architectural treasures of their local town. Since Devizes is full of such treasures, it was a delight to compile this new collection. We hope you will enjoy it.

Beverley and Tim Jollands
Weavern Books

*The Crammer pond lies between the churchyard of St James, Southbroom,
and the Green, traditional site of the town's fairs.*

# Introduction

SET AMONG QUIET green hills and plains in the very centre of Wiltshire, Devizes is a town that owes its site, name, status and layout to its castle. But while the town pays tribute in its coat of arms to this iconic building – described by the 12th-century chronicler Henry of Huntingdon as 'the most splendid in Europe' – no medieval towers crown the impressive castle mound today. The original lines of its defences, however, are still clearly visible in the D-shaped medieval street plan that survives remarkably unaltered in the town centre. And there is still a castle to complete the scene, although it is a Victorian fantasy rather than a Norman stronghold.

There is no mention of a settlement at this location in Domesday Book, but the adjoining manors of Rowde, Cannings and Potterne do appear, and on a spur of high ground where their boundaries met the castle was sited, probably by Osmund, Bishop of Salisbury, around 1080. This was the *castrum ad divisas* – the 'castle at the boundaries' – that gave the town laid out around its walls its intriguing plural name. It was still known as 'The Devizes' in the Victorian era, and the variations 'Vises', 'Vies' and 'the Vyse' were all in use from the 14th century.

When Osmund's wooden structure burnt down in 1113, a more ambitious replacement was built in stone by the succeeding bishop, Roger of Salisbury. Roger had been Henry I's chancellor and the power and wealth he accrued were said to be second only to the king's. After Henry's death in 1135 the struggle for the throne between his daughter Matilda and her cousin Stephen led to nearly two decades of civil war, in which Roger's huge fortress played a strategic role. Though Stephen had the support of the bishops, in 1139 he seized the possessions of his over-mighty ally Roger of Salisbury, including Devizes Castle. Despite its brief capture by the mercenary Robert Fitzhubert, who was in turn captured and hanged by Stephen, the castle thus became a royal possession.

*The Market Cross, designed by Benjamin Wyatt, was erected in 1814,*
*and is still surrounded by market stalls every Thursday.*

Matilda, who had most of her support in the southwest, besieged and won the castle in 1141 with the help of the local people, and held court there until 1148.

It was from Matilda that Devizes obtained a charter in 1141, relieving it of trade tariffs and thus allowing markets to be held. The evocatively named Monday Market Street leads to the original market place near the parish church of St Mary, where a market cross stood near what is now the White Bear Inn. There is evidence for a Thursday market from the reign of Henry III; it still bustles every week in the present-day Market Place, which occupies a site that would originally have been inside the outer bailey of the castle. When the castle's strategic importance declined after 1300 its defences were abandoned and the town was able to expand into this central space.

In the medieval markets the goods of local leatherworkers – skinners, tanners, glovers and shoemakers – were prominent, but from the 14th century the cloth trade gradually grew to become the mainstay of the town's economy, as merchants switched from exporting fine-quality English fleeces to the weaving centres of Europe and instead traded in home-produced woven cloth. The local white broadcloth was celebrated as the 'blanket of the Vies', and the clothiers who controlled the weavers' work and sold the finished cloth made large fortunes. Writing in the late 17th century, the traveller Celia Fiennes described Devizes as 'A very neate little town with a very good market house and town hall sett on stone pillars; it is a bourrough and a very rich tradeing place ffor the Clothing trade.'

By the time of her visit the castle was no more. During the Civil War the Parliamentarians had regarded Devizes as a significant prize, because it stood between Charles I's headquarters in Oxford and his support base in the West Country. A Parliamentary force led by William Waller besieged the town in July 1643 (the scars of their shot can be seen in the walls of St John's church) but it held out. When the Royalist cavalry arrived to relieve the siege it routed Waller's force in the battle of Roundway Down to the north of the town, pursuing the fleeing enemy horse over a hidden precipice into what has since been known as the 'Bloody Ditch'. However, in 1645 Cromwell himself arrived to besiege the castle, bombarding it from the Market Place; it was surrendered and ordered to be 'slighted', or demolished. In the 18th century two windmills stood on the castle mound, used for grinding rape seed and later snuff. The brick base of one of the mills was incorporated into the present gothic pastiche, begun in 1842 for the Leach family, and now divided into private homes.

Though the town lost its medieval castle, its churches withstood bombardment. Both St Mary's and the even more splendid St John's, whose parish is thought to have included the castle while St Mary's served the townspeople, date from the 12th century and retain their Norman chancels as well as the glamorous 15th-century additions financed by wealthy burgesses. Devizes' third medieval church tower (the rest of the

LEFT *Brownston House, New Park Street (1720) and St Mary's church.*
RIGHT *16 Market Place, the home of John Kent MP from 1619.*

building is Victorian) is that of St James, founded as the chapel of a 13th-century leper hospital outside the town in Southbroom. It overlooks the Green and the Crammer, or town pond. The latter claims to be the setting for the Wiltshire legend of the Moonrakers – a group of smugglers who hid their contraband French brandy in the pond. When an excise man caught them one night, rakes in hand, retrieving the kegs, the men feigned stupidity and pointed to the reflection of the moon in the water, convincing him they were trying to catch the 'gurt cheese'.

The town's fortunes continued to rest on woollen cloth in the 18th century, by which time it was specializing in the production of hard-wearing serge and a lighter fabric known as drugget. The prominent clothier John Anstie also supplied more prosperous customers in London and Europe with a fine-quality twill suiting called cassimere. Breaking with the tradition of farming out piecework to the local weavers in

*A tympanum sculpture (1998) by Eric Stanford, over the door of John Anstie's factory, illustrates processes in the manufacture of woollen cloth.*

their cottages, around 1785 he built a factory in New Park Street, in which he installed twenty spinning jennies and some three hundred looms. The Anstie family also had interests in brewing and tobacco, two other major trades in Devizes, which continued to flourish long after its cloth businesses had lost out to more heavily industrialized centres of production. While the once fashionable snuff survives here only in a street name, beer is still a major presence. Wadworth's imposing Northgate Brewery has dominated the northern end of the Market Place since 1885, and its shire horses still clop along the streets every week making deliveries to the town pubs.

Devizes' markets and fairs brought in considerable trade in wool, corn and livestock, and were an important source of civic revenue. By the mid-18th century there were two direct coach routes between London and Bath, one of which passed through Devizes, bringing the fashionable world to its numerous inns. The growing affluence of the town attracted professionals such as doctors and lawyers, and its first bank opened in 1775. The men of substance commissioned elegant houses for themselves, but mainly built them in locally produced brick rather than the more desirable Bath stone, which had to be carted uphill at great expense and was therefore usually reserved for the most visible, decorative parts – doorcases, cornices and quoins. It is the beautiful handmade bricks, however, finely rubbed and skilfully laid, with their subtle gradations of warm colour, that give the town its distinctive character.

Although much of the town centre has an 18th-century appearance, a number of its graceful Georgian façades conceal older, timber-framed buildings, brought up to date by their fashion-conscious owners with stuccoed fronts and new sash windows. In some cases, such as the jettied range in St John's Court, the update is obvious, but new fronts were also applied to timber-framed houses in Long Street and even the old Bridewell (now the Grange) in Bridewell Street, which served as the town jail from 1579 until 1836.

New public buildings went up too, and for these stone was not considered too extravagant. The New Hall (now the Old Town Hall) in Wine Street was built in 1752, originally as a market hall with an open piazza at street level, and was designed by a local architect. For the new Town Hall in St John's Street, however, a more celebrated designer was employed – Thomas Baldwin, Bath City Surveyor and one of the leading architects of the Georgian city. The Town Hall was opened in 1808 with a grand ball, held in its elegant first-floor assembly room under a ceiling decorated in the style of Robert Adam.

By the time the imposing Assize Court in Northgate Street was built in 1835, to a classical design by T. H. Wyatt, the cost of Bath stone had fallen dramatically following the opening of the Kennet and Avon canal. Begun in 1794 to connect Bristol with London by linking the Avon with the Kennet, which flows into the Thames at Reading, the canal was finally

*The Town Hall of 1808, with its graceful bow front, was a substantial remodelling of the 17th-century Wool Hall to a design by Thomas Baldwin.*

completed in 1810 by the 29 locks that raised the cut by 72 metres in just over 3 km up Caen Hill. James Waylen's 1839 *Chronicles of the Devizes* describes the Caen Hill flight as a 'great work of art' and mentions the striking night-time vista of 'the long descending line of gas lamps which here protect the passage'.

As well as halving the cost of transporting stone, the canal connected Devizes with the Somerset coalfield, and Devizes Wharf became a distribution depot for coal. Barges brought tobacco from Bristol and carried beer to London. But when the Great Western Railway was completed in 1841, providing a faster and cheaper method of carrying

*The railway line from Devizes to Hungerford ran under the castle mound;*
*the tunnel was bricked up when the line closed in 1966.*

coal, the canal's receipts plummeted. The GWR acquired it in 1852 and
after 1873 left it to fall into disrepair. But the route for the main Bristol to
London railway line ran through Swindon and Chippenham, so Devizes
did not get its own rail connection until 1857, when a branch line was
built from Holt Junction. A westward extension to Hungerford, which
involved tunnelling under the castle mound, was opened in 1862, finally
linking the town with London.

The Devizes branch line was closed in 1966, but the derelict canal was
given a reprieve, thanks to years of volunteer effort. It reopened in 1990
and is now frequented by holidaymakers, walkers, cyclists and wildlife.
The only boats in a hurry to reach London these days are the canoes
taking part in the 200-km race from Devizes to Westminster, which has
taken place every Easter since 1948.

# A Photographic Treasure Hunt

*1*

2

3

4

5

6

*7*

8

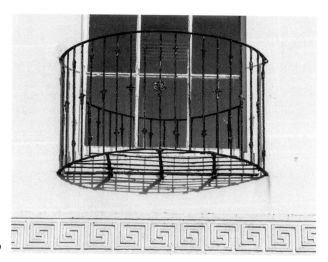

9

*10*

11

*12*

13

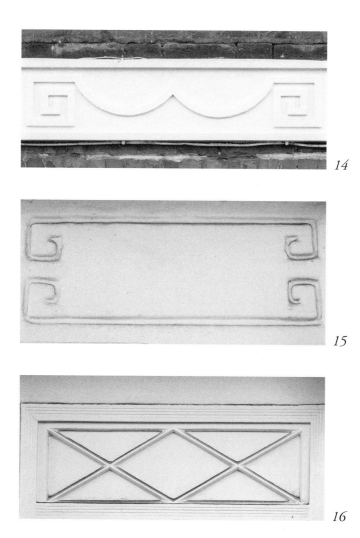

*14*

*15*

*16*

*17*

*18*

19

*20*

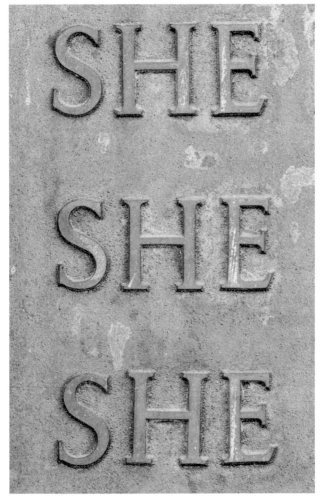

21

22

23

24

*25*

*26*

27

28

29

*30*

31

*32*

33

*34*

*35*

*36*

*37*

*38*

39

*40*

41

42

*43*

*44*

45

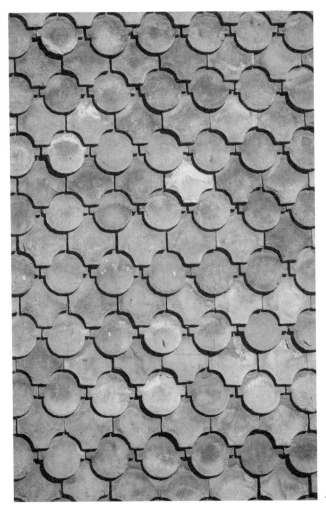

46

THOMAS HASSALL,
WHO DIED AUG 2? 1873,
AGED 54 YEARS.
FOR 22 YEARS MASTER OF THE
DEVIZES UNION WORKHOUSE.
ALSO
MARY HIS WIDOW,
WHO DIED JANUARY 18, 1876,
AGED 55 YEARS.
FOR 24 YEARS MATRON OF THE
DEVIZES UNION WORKHOUSE.

47

*48*

49

*50*

*51*

*52*

*53*

54

*55*

56

57

58

59

*60*

*61*

62

63

64

65

66

67

68

*69*

*70*

*71*

*72*

73

74

75

76

77

*78*

*79*

80

81

*82*

*83*

*84*

*85*

86

87

88

89

*90*

*91*

*92*

*93*

94

95

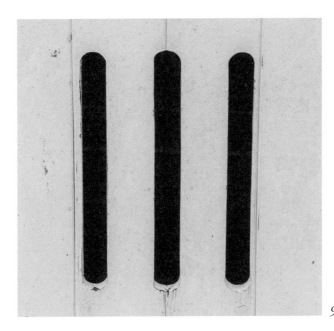

96

97

*98*

99

*100*

# Acknowledgements

The publishers and photographer are grateful to the following for their help in bringing this project to fruition:

PRINCIPAL SPONSOR
Hunter French Estate Agents (1st prize)

PARTNERS
Devizes Books
Devizes Town Council
Wiltshire Museum (Devizes)

PATRONS
Ultra-Warm Plumbing & Heating Engineers (2nd prize)
Wansbroughs Solicitors (3rd prize)
Devizes Fine Kitchens
The Flemish Weaver (Corsham)
No 59
Original Glory
The Peppermill
The Wharf Tea Rooms

*Links to all of the above can be found on
our website, weavernbooks.co.uk.*

## About the Photographer

Andy Rose was born and brought up in Corsham, where his family has been rooted since the 19th century. On leaving school, he travelled the world as a merchant seaman. Returning to his home town, he spent the next twenty-eight years as a postman – twelve as a part-time firefighter – before becoming a manager at The Flemish Weaver.

Photography has been Andy's abiding passion, with a particular interest in travel and documentary. A 2014 trip to the Arctic culminated in an exhibition at the Mall Galleries, London, while a trip to India honed a keen eye for portraiture, as evidenced in his first book, *When Poldark Came to Corsham*.

Andy's next project, *Corsham in Focus*, enabled him to focus on form, texture, pattern, tone, light and contrast, elements brought into sharp relief in black-and-white photography. He came across architectural details that he had never noticed before, and resonances with his family's long association with the town. The book-cum-treasure-hunt caught on, and Devizes – with its architectural treasures – was a natural choice for Andy's second collection of elusive images.

Andy Rose Photography
7 Church Street, Corsham, Wiltshire SN13 0BY
www.andyrosephoto.com

# Rules of the Competition

Entries must be submitted on the original, detachable entry form found at the back of the book; photocopies will not be accepted. If short of space, you can attach additional sheets of paper to complete your answers. Please write clearly. Locations should be precisely identified and your descriptions unambiguous: for example, if the image is of a chimney pot and the house has several, say which one is shown as well as giving the address. The judges' decision will be final.

All forms must be delivered to Weavern Books, 29 High Street, Corsham SN13 0EZ, by midnight on 31 October 2018. If you would like confirmation of receipt, please include your email address. The answers will be revealed and the winners announced at a prize-giving ceremony at the Wiltshire Museum on Friday 23 November 2018. (Thereafter, answers will be available online at www.weavernbooks.co.uk.)

There will be a first prize of £500 donated by Hunter French, a second prize of £250 donated by Ultra-Warm, and a third prize of £150 donated by Wansbroughs Solicitors. In the event of more than one complete and correct solution being received, the names of the successful competitors will be entered in a draw to determine the prizewinners. If there are no complete entries but two or more with the same number of correct answers there will also be a draw.

The names of the top 100 entrants will also go into a draw for raffle prizes donated by our Patrons, so it is worthwhile entering even if you feel you haven't found enough answers to win one of the main prizes.

The publishers and the photographer, and their families, may not enter the competition.

Though every attempt has been made to avoid this, the publishers cannot accept responsibility for any discrepancies between the photographs and the subjects as a result of changes at the locations following publication.

# *Checklist*

| | | | | | | | |
|---|---|---|---|---|---|---|---|
| 1 | | 26 | | 51 | | 76 | |
| 2 | | 27 | | 52 | | 77 | |
| 3 | | 28 | | 53 | | 78 | |
| 4 | | 29 | | 54 | | 79 | |
| 5 | | 30 | | 55 | | 80 | |
| 6 | | 31 | | 56 | | 81 | |
| 7 | | 32 | | 57 | | 82 | |
| 8 | | 33 | | 58 | | 83 | |
| 9 | | 34 | | 59 | | 84 | |
| 10 | | 35 | | 60 | | 85 | |
| 11 | | 36 | | 61 | | 86 | |
| 12 | | 37 | | 62 | | 87 | |
| 13 | | 38 | | 63 | | 88 | |
| 14 | | 39 | | 64 | | 89 | |
| 15 | | 40 | | 65 | | 90 | |
| 16 | | 41 | | 66 | | 91 | |
| 17 | | 42 | | 67 | | 92 | |
| 18 | | 43 | | 68 | | 93 | |
| 19 | | 44 | | 69 | | 94 | |
| 20 | | 45 | | 70 | | 95 | |
| 21 | | 46 | | 71 | | 96 | |
| 22 | | 47 | | 72 | | 97 | |
| 23 | | 48 | | 73 | | 98 | |
| 24 | | 49 | | 74 | | 99 | |
| 25 | | 50 | | 75 | | 100 | |

| 71 | |
|----|---|
| 72 | |
| 73 | |
| 74 | |
| 75 | |
| 76 | |
| 77 | |
| 78 | |
| 79 | |
| 80 | |
| 81 | |
| 82 | |
| 83 | |
| 84 | |
| 85 | |
| 86 | |
| 87 | |
| 88 | |
| 89 | |
| 90 | |

| 91 | |
|-----|--|
| 92 | |
| 93 | |
| 94 | |
| 95 | |
| 96 | |
| 97 | |
| 98 | |
| 99 | |
| 100 | |

*with thanks to our patrons*

1st prize
£500

2nd prize
£250

3rd prize
£150